RACHAEL HANIBLE

AMBER'S

Magical Savings Box

First Interactive Lesson on Earning and Saving Money!

AuthorHouse™
1663 Liberty Drive
Bloomington, IN 47403
www.authorhouse.com
Phone: 1 (800) 839-8640

Published by AuthorHouse 03/24/2018

ISBN: 978-1-5462-3444-9 (sc)
ISBN: 978-1-5462-3443-2 (e)

Library of Congress Control Number: 2018903647

Print information available on the last page.

authorHOUSE®

This Savings Book belongs to

Autumn

Believe in you! Reach for the Stars! Rachelle

<u>Dedication</u>

Amber
I still love you just the same, our connection goes beyond space, time and physical presence. You still make me cry, laugh and dance.... Still...
October 11th 2001 – June 12th 2005

Ma
Remember the fake money you gave me when I was 6? I would sit for hours counting and adding zeros on the end. I gave you fake money to pay real bills (Ha).
That sparked something in me.
Look at me now.
Look at you now.
God is amazing!
Thank you for everything!

One day in Amber's class, the kids started talking about a new toy.

They were so excited because this wasn't just an ordinary toy.

This toy was MAGICAL!

Amber seemed to be one of the few kids who didn't have this new toy at home.

Amber went to the mall with
her Aunt one day.

Amber loves their mall trips because
she loves seeing all the beautiful
and colorful people there.

While walking, they passed by a store with an awesome display case in the window.

"Look, Auntie! That's the magical toy!

All the kids in school have one!
Can we buy it? Pretty please?!"
Amber yelled.

"Looks like that toy costs $12.

Do you have $12, Amber?"
her Aunt asked.

"Not yet, but I will find a way
to get it!" Amber replied.

They grabbed some ice cream just before leaving the mall.

Amber thought about that toy the whole ride home.

That night, Amber found an old shoe box and decorated it with all of her favorite things.

Hearts, butterflies, stars, and a few rainbows covered the box.

Amber called it

"The Magical Savings Box."

The next morning, Amber got up bright and early to offer her mom some help around the house before school in exchange for $1.

After school, Amber helped with setting the table for 50¢.

Amber's mom gave her an extra $1.25 for helping to clean the dishes and put them away.

How much does Amber have so far in her Magical Savings Box?

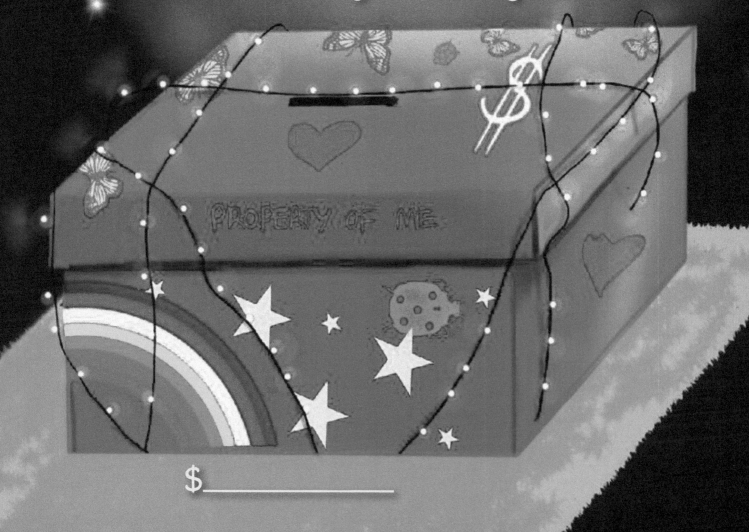

$_____

The next day Amber heard her
Dad outside working on the car.

She ran outside asking her dad
if he needed any help.

That day Amber earned $3 handing her dad tools and bringing him lemonade.

During one of her weekend trips to grandma's house, Amber helped her grand mom at the super market and while preparing Sunday Dinner.

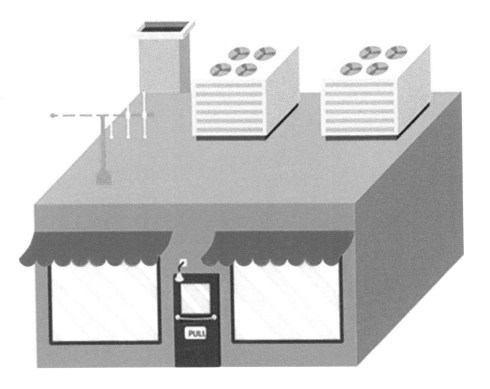

Just before she left, she realized her grand mom put money in her pocket.

On the ride home, she reached into her pocket and noticed her grand mom gave her 5 WHOLE DOLLARS!

She yelled,
"Wow! Thanks, Grand mom!"

PROPERTY OF ME

How much does Amber have now?

$_____

How much money does Amber
need to meet her goal?

$_____

Amber was so excited once she realized
how close she was to her goal!

Write a note to Amber congratulating her on all her hard work so far below.

_____

_____

_____

_____

_____

She searched all over her house, looking for things to do and ways to help her parents to earn more money.

Amber started dusting, sweeping, and even helped her mom with her baby brother.

Before her bedtime story,
Amber's mom thanked her for all
her help and then gave her $2.

Amber couldn't control her excitement.

She jumped up to do the happy dance on the bed.

How much does Amber have now?

$_____

The next time Amber heard her Aunt was going to the mall, she couldn't wait to ask to ride along.

"Auntie! Auntie! I have the money for the Magical Toy!"

"Really Amber? How did you get the money?" Her Aunt asked.

"Working Hard and saving a lot!" Amber replied.

When Amber pulled her money
out to count, she realized she lost
a dollar somewhere, somehow.
This made Amber very sad.

Can you write a special note to Amber to cheer her up?

_____

_____

_____

_____

_____

_____

_____

_____

How much money does Amber have now?

$_____

After seeing Amber's disappointment, her Aunt gave her $1 and thanked her for always keeping her company at the mall.

They went into the store.

Amber ran to grab the toy and

paid for it with her own money.

She felt like a big girl.

Amber couldn't wait to get home to show Mom, Dad, and all the other kids what she had been working so hard for.

You too can have that wonderful feeling Amber had over and over again.

Just set a goal for that Magical thing
you want, work hard, earn money,
and save until you reach your goal.
Make sure you share the importance
of saving with your friends so they
can have Magical things too!

My name is

_____

_____

When I grow up I want to be a

_____

_____

_____

_____

Because (write reasons)

_____

_____

_____

_____

_____

I would like to give money to

_____

_____

For (write reasons)

_____

_____

_____

_____

_____

I would like to save (enter amount)

_____

I believe in myself.

I am smart.

I am talented.

All of my dreams can come true.

I believe that if I work hard and save I
can buy all the magical things I need.

My First Savings Journal

Example: <u>Today grand mom gave me $5 for my birthday.</u>

_____

_____

_____

_____

_____

_____

_____

_____

CPSIA information can be obtained
at www.ICGtesting.com
Printed in the USA
BVHW020337110719
553176BV00012B/22/P